Booker
a collection
Vol.I

A.W.Booker

Copyright © 2025 Alec Booker

ISBN: 978-1-917778-32-9

All rights reserved, including the right to reproduce this book, or portions thereof in any form. No part of this text may be reproduced, transmitted, downloaded, decompiled, reverse engineered, or stored, in any form or introduced into any information storage and retrieval system, in any form or by any means, whether electronic or mechanical without the express written permission of the author.

Acknowledgement

Not in wit nor jest, I would like to acknowledge acknowledgment in concept for without such what judgement would I hold but mere thought, lacked process.

Bounded by waves of events, must find me in process, in process of thought subsequent of which spills from the mind in form of worded transform.

For those too in path of life, another acknowledgment, to all fellow travellers, might we wonder.

And in wonder should we wander, I acknowledge my feet in wit, not in jest.

Blisters certainly do not bear banter.

The acknowledgement for jest is allured to life alone.

What humour you seem to settle by curse or cure, in chance of coin.

I do acknowledge my mother

A beautiful soul

As do I know

Painted by Morn'

I lay in bed, awoken by none.
Tossed for all I could. No more. I'll start.
Before dawn, morning colours are hatching
such that I must view, climb to the
window three stories high.
And behold, three wanderers, high.
Through my telescope, I glimpse at each
peacefully and in miss, I see the giant,
the red rock and the married.
I should miss this rise, no clouds to float.
Coated, I walk by. Now wanderers fade but
colours are stretched. Deep red to
mustard orange, sky green to blue beyond.
The skyrise is at peaking view.
A shadowed crane attempts to pick the sun fruit.
Concrete towers, closer houses, closest a tree line
to spy through. Birds from pigeons to pheasants join
in flight or in call. Crisp breath housed peace.
It's quiet, it's morning. No, it's quiet, there's a plague.
This would take it all away, colourful morn'.

-25 March'20-

Ag Caint le Préachán an Diabhail

These purgatory crossroads would me lost

for I cannot read the signs

so for the most, I randomly adhere.

Perhaps this way, coaxed on by the Devil's crow.

Why not? I have no better guidance

and what for my own but no more than

loose lit tunnels where even the ghost plays

part in fear. Have it not been in

my place, I would have succeeded.

I learnt the dark lust of night with ease.

An evil befriending but I needed to be

here. Without this dark, who but God might

say there was ever light.

Walk with the Devil, let them speak.

Here you learn how you are.

-March'20-

Glance Now

Upon the midst of life in pleasure

might plea in hands of vain,

knoweth, shan't will hold.

Stringed loose joys

that happen by gust,

enter life in time by front.

Shouldn't fault natural passing,

I shall.

Forgive me when I too revert,

I hide not much.

Clasp in tort, most baneful of sly,

these drawless soul affairs,

dined wilfully, knoweth, held will shall.

Ought is not must, in does I

fail here, then so fail should I find.

-5 Dec'24-

Mind Love

Love would not be as love would seem.

Fallacy.

I bid off lust and jealousy.

What more do I have?

An adaptation of pure: Joy, Trust, Care.

Take IT out of account!

I shout it: Take IT Out of Account!

Love does not bear physicality of dance

nor looks which heed primal sixth senses. What knack.

To love is to do so by minds of thoughts.

No more, no less.

I'll mind.

-undated-

I, Which Sleep

I wish to fall asleep someday

in which I dream no more

to loath these hours of constant pain

I wince out from the core.

-undated-

A Boat for Hire

Drift aloft these waters calm,
deep navy blue does arc the sky.
Need not us know the time of day
for when here a-bask
time nor day are concepts of interest
instead a contrast far stay in prime
of which we talk for hours.
You and I, the sailor folk
not just for the raft of which we float
but sailors of the mind's deep
and deeper do I find my mind on you.
Like capt'n's orders past soft blue
as do the sails catch wind a'sea,
I too have caught a force of three.
Hull to keel, connection holds.
Compass to hand, points to home.
And as for the last might we consider
a game of tennis eyed by skipper
and forever I shall score not
one point.

-Taunton Sept'23-

No. 60

The man fishing [insert known fish] doesn't

seem to mind.

Can he even see the bridge?

Can he even hear the bridge?

Does anyone hear the bridge?? Or haveth

the madness set in?

No, that be my original sin

a coin of which double sided.

Ruddy noisy bridge.

-Lisbon Dec'24-

Nightful Ponder

I lay in bed with nicotine between fingers.

My barrack's dorm window open as the heat lingers.

Thoughts of mind about future lane.

Contemplation of past and pain.

It's a trail of one that the path is set

to bestow the dream of hope isn't to regret.

For we must all get on with feelings behind

though best to think and thus remind.

It's not only the present which plays effect

but the past to form a future we reflect.

As old as I manage

I want to look back at my back.

Look back and let flow the emotions

around life with all its commotions.

And as I stub my intake out

I'll remember the aspects of which I'm about.

-undated-

Woeful of Another's Woo

If I weren't to sip this pain,
this pain of sorrow,
would not my vows of lay be just.
In heed I blaze fort'.
Not other in night shall seek nor see.
Tainted which the clouds fluster,
bent blinded by your cleave.
Oh, love of your sheep,
cherish but fallen.
Path wades.
Do you send me to punish?
For I shall take it.
Oh love, hooved cloak.
The better of me, taken.
But seedeth you may wonder.
My soul,
be it strained and numb,
I shall take the burden
and heed me,
my cares would last for so long.

-undated-

Photomeleto

Ask simply and it shall not be.

Fundamental aspects of the continuum.

This holds sure,

a transfer of energy, thenbeit.

Come rise, before set, I sense you.

Boiled pot of self time stew, you release.

Even to my essential of lamp and radio, you're present.

Are you awake? What more mysteries

must you hold? The grasp for power

is far further than a quick conclusion.

I feel you to be more even in description,

not pail fed complexities.

Like natural progression, no rush here

but lullaby your solutions to me, dearly.

-undated-

jEnder

Assignments of tainted labels

yet seemly town of gender,

orientation dependent on

which card given.

Stop.

We are what we are

base this on will.

Do you wish to be strong as an bullock or weak as a hen

in simple structure of argue.

Pity you if you see gender here,

define your words.

Right will does not care for

your reproductive body.

Craveth you soul in hope

you are well. This is all that matters.

-undated-

No. 50

Pages of lustre,

for what more do you need cry for

but the bottle in your hand.

Peace he willed

I have adored in prior fine light.

You would be lost if it would be to

forget your own hand.

Love yourself more so than any could.

-undated-

No. 31

We swear quite gently,

these days.

At toes for our dress

no time, these days.

A marriage is a game

not chess but gamble,

these days.

A beg, a pardon,

a pungent o"ffairs

All in the name of good grief.

-undated-

The Cobwebs of Memories

Woven and wrinkled,

outstretched across wall entirety,

not more to collect than dust laden.

Once out fret with purposed nature.

Attire which loathes such speak.

Nine years would hold but such.

Disturbance abundance, a common laugh.

Here the web lays still,

no touch nor feather could

blush to hear,

until house stone collapses.

-undated-

No. 41

Confusion but pure understanding,

I hear you.

~ you are me, how could you

let this happen! ~

To me

~ I am you?

Then you are me.

Are you me? ~

To which I feel and know, I am not.

A punch, a quibble, he throws

the coffee out of my hand.

~ I will not be you

for you will be no more.

What change haveth?

But now you shall fade ~

Shame it, I shan't blame my past.

-undated-

No. 40

As we morally walk towards the shame,

concern to curiosity be I.

At end, we are here, stand forth.

I, alike me, find in which there are

no pleadings to uptake.

Wince as to what am I angry at him.

~ I, you.. it's.. ~

I cannot hold grudge, and I don't.

~How could you have let this outcome?~

I wish to say.

-undated-

An Out of Love Rant

Bah, what is love

but controlled sex.

Lust before wisdom,

a coffee should ought me better.

Find a flower that f*cks

with your nose.

Eat the petals, but not just,

the thorned stem too.

Ouch does which this slow sorrow

fade into the background.

Pollution of life.

Quite sour.

Quite out of love,

Perhaps this is why.

I shan't lose all my sleep.

-Taunton April'23-

No. 35

Ouf for which I've hurt you.

Does it cool the burdened witch to know that I feel pain.

Or need I strip the sheets that lay me.

Eat well as I do want, kissed that founded end.

I neither want hate nor toil upon this garden o'joy.

Hear Me When I Say

Does your soul seek'th lurt?

Or can you cold wash these nigh shadows.

For I, for which have known no limits even under stars.

Forgotten is the wind that lusts for I shall not be lost.

But be it rowboat in dismay,

we learn, we love, we fight together

until death finds our way.

-Taunton 6 Oct'20-

Might We Travel

Top deck,

my shadow cast on waved water.

I hold to my hat gripped tight.

Clear sky to gaze on,

Orion points to the growing moon.

Land before I set,

bidbaid my farewells.

May lead wings be clipped,

shoes worn,

paths ventured.

I hold dear to my hat,

journeys behold.

For when they ask

'Where is home?'

I do so boldly answer

'Might we travel'

-Feb'20-

No. 39

I teleport back,

back before,

before army or toil had hit such youth.

As I walk past

~ Alec, you plum, let's go ~

I, be him, climb over the short green fence.

We walk towards the dark, towards the water well, in fact.

I reach out my hand in jest to hold.

We do.

He claims no more than deaf would speak.

I, in silence,

no smite but grimace.

-undated-

No. 42

The old sleepy man

of grudge and bane.

Bane of no man to haveth.

Eugh.

He were me,

me of passed youth yet yonder age

becomes nay of thanks.

I shall change, be it now.

Nay thanks.

Not Lord knows I shall change.

Be it for my control.

Control of this Humour.

-undated-

Hoped

No thought nor care

unless we wish to make the

unfortunate bond.

No wish be always forfeit in bane,

here flutter to aches and scornship.

Scars to not be tampered nor mended.

Prepare to aware the unworthy ghoul

and lay bare the petals of lust.

Through fear we dine merrily.

By your hand,

not mine.

-undated-

Shed Moth

Would not want the moth
to be outside.
A flutter on the pane,
a lead of straight,
a lead of lead.
The shed would hold
them well.
Harboured from the rain
but wants would out
and out wood wants
does the moth need.
Though I ponder
as watched on moth,
I ought not know if rain
succumbs our late cousin.
In instant I shall idle on
this act of freedom
as might just be in vain
in hind to accept desire in the rain.

-Taunton July'23-

No. 7

Feel within,

the emotion which called.

Out t'which not known.

Ouf, you deeds,

deed demons

I cannot hold.

Lacked me of your chains

but willed me of mine.

You hadn't me of lust,

we lost you far more than

the pence to be tilled.

Paid me,

watch slim,

I will prevail.

-undated-

No. 6

If I were on one knee hence now,

what would truthful say you tell?

Would you forgive the laid in prior

and move on to eternity?

A feeling up turned, what for it?

But Ouf!, crashing bane.

A feeling of pure liability.

Had not you felt me out to which you owe,

I might not propose

but rather bask in grave solemn.

A love which burns in ounce by toe,

believe it of fade, I hold deep.

In not sole purpose to break your oaths

but too to lay the whisp of ships,

laden ships of burn.

Here, my ashes.

Live lightly

or love not at all.

-undated-

Morn'g With You

Crescent moon, you shadow well

and might appoint you does follow suit.

I find you to the hillside

where rest here we shall see.

Juvenile sky, you had me watched.

Hear, sound it, the birds will tell you.

A lonely cat thumps sourly as you make sight of prowl.

There flowers morn'g with you, grant you for Her grace.

Lion sun, you paint grey clouds rose-gold.

Spill rush, grand glory.

Your colours, lustre of this land.

Hold m'hand, we'll walk home together.

-May'20-

Lay Wit on Walks

Over the mountains back
in a post dusk sky
I watch my town.
Lights stitched in chaotic order,
the constellation of home.
Back turned to the field below
I make my descent.
There's a wire here
but it is too dark to follow!
Hat to hand, I wave it in front.
Please blessed it shall a-warn me.
But thought,
if I were blind, I would still
not be shocked
for if disadvantage lays before you,
does not mean you lay to fail.
Hear it, sound. Touch to sight.
Forgotten are the witless.

-16 Jan'21-

The Comfort of Despair

Of which I am forth with a blatant mask of joy.
I hold dear to smile, an illusion much so my
mind would rest at ease and believe.
The scorned crown I wear as weighted
to feather. Heath it, I shall crawl.
Perhaps sleep is the answer.
I fail to see the hardship. I accept the
pain as my duty to find truth outside.
Blindfolded, I wish to cross this swamp,
my heart is to explore, my mind to ponder.
I crave help but wish to reject it at the
slight arrival. I hold my own hand.

-Dec'19-

At First Spring Evening

Gust easily moves dial west to east.

An early sunset, much sky to paint.

Appeal I, no more.

I can see you etch.

Ah, what belief to see this colour.

Such not warm but cold in fair piece.

I have dearly missed a happy end day,

cold drink my company.

We cook tonight, laugh, be merry.

Regardless what we did,

essence of peace.

-undated-

To Which We Siblings Are

Here we stand as kin, forth life
but toil different paths
to say not which you, mine, have moved
in solemn moral ways.
Gracious is the morning sun
but not a mere does this compare
the influence you had on such my journey.
You, I, we differ more
than turtle to dove
but I heed in such a proclaim.
Out holding time does such more
than earthly summons, parted would
a blessed bond.
Hear as I grant you grace
for without your guide would I, turmoiled,
in exchange your compassion, here lay my love.
Forth loath, we stand as kin
forever once and forever more.

-undated-

No. 26

My friend,

let's light a campfire.

Let rest our orchard thoughts

that I have yours

and you mine.

We'll not agree

but instead

ponder under oath.

Why might you kindle such blame?

Here shores sort short sures.

Listen,

we are but two

housed by one,

not nature nor toil

but hope.

-April'20-

God Heed You

Let us run away together,
folded hand in hand.
You and I,
the moon lit skies,
'til boon inks lay to dry.
It takes a plenty does this heel
of which we claim to fold.
You and I,
the mountain rise,
watch as oceans sigh.
Creak which not the narrow say
but heedeth when to act,
we'll not speak then this oath of joy
but tailor throats to whisper.
Waned would see the overthrow,
our solemn arcs to throne.
You and I,
the morning men,
yet 'til these motions die.

-30 April'20-

Cloud Traffic

Cold night at gaze a clouded sky.
Typical sigh but natural position posed.
I stare as though there were stars.
A stiff smoke to melt today. Needed.
Right glance.
The end of the cloud? I see a gap.
Stars bright, constellations gleam
as though the first page of a book, opened.
Come on, light cloud, part more.
As if the lord had quenched his fire,
drifted the cloud, smoke screen.
Blissful night now of stars design.
How I could watch onwards,
hope opened in a scene of thought dull.
Right glance.
The start of another cloud.
Ah, enjoyed while it lasted.
Greet you, grey lit white,
you shan't last for long.

-Feb'20-

Your Pities, I Have None

To have me bathed and clothed in subtle ways
as if I had not seen the shadow caster.
I lay blatant, naked and crippled on your
cobble streets.
Arrest me, for I have no shame,
my time shall flow regardless.
Your dark tunnels, I have lit with
my bloodied eyes, sour illumination
and in turn, I fear not, exempt
willed, the fear of my innocence lost
once more by your coal black hands.
Might you win, can you lose?
My might forbade such winnings as
would in practice.
But tried willed, I am here.

-Taunton July'20-

Afloat Drift Down

You lost the plot

before I even knew you,

poor soul of man.

How deep the abyss

might you fall humbly.

Knocks forward flaunts,

towers downward.

Hope hear the calls

which laid below, find you.

I am but your soul bound.

And though we might venture

but'f crash,

is all up onto you.

-Exeter'24-

In Journey to King's Humble

It has become dark quickly.
My fear, I will not be able to see
nor taste victory in result.
Heed me, do help.
Which way do I turn
and where might I place my head.
What labours.
Forget not your hinder,
alight it on your shoulders.
Brace you as I will me
that I shan't cover; I aggress.
Here on, the light twilights.
Bid all, not one as we are.
I take the Lord's hand in fade.
You shall be alright, I'm brief.
Care as I should, live well.
And above all, abode your heart
pleasantly in a king's humble,
my love.

-17 April'20-

Not to Be Scared

A thought beyond discord,
be thou it,
you'll be.
Let lowe' your qualms.
Hoist, now!
Here you are
beyond speech.
But heed be it flow.
Forth on a heaven cleave
be it all in your nigh.
Eat all worded pains,
you will surrender to forward banes few
or see with blunder that
it heaves you not to speak.
But speak for it, not thyself,
you baneful spirit.
Here comes your bread
non laid with care.

-'20-

No. 14

What cares you.

I beg it's you.

Simplest no more

than earth and care maketh you.

No more.

Divide your character.

Divide once more.

Denominate by x by 1.

What haveth but care.

Mind this but ask;

what ought you do on to your cares?

-22 April'21-

A Poem for Mars

Gone these days

that ought be forgotten,

laden with our debt.

Debt of depth in outer reach

which mindsets wail to wade.

Heaven's belief, this art I believe,

good grief do I not fear pain.

Yet pain of fear, which fear does lurk,

chains me to such fiction.

Fiction here,

an assortment of heirs

moulded by much mind.

Mind which might then mould these heirs in fiction from the pain.

Stance before the flower bed,

in thought my debt be paid.

-29 Dec'21-

Author notes

My laptop battery is near to running dry so if I cut off, you know why. Valid excuse for briefness.

It's late, as I'd claim. 11pm is late. Those younger than 31 may disagree but I do not. Work tomorrow, I am trying my best not to text back a friend's ex. I do not change, though I probably should. Love affairs do me well. As well as a morning shock of shame.

I should sleep, 23:04, 22% battery. 2% awake.

I note this isn't relevant in any hand but mumbling of the present ..which in sleight is still a note by the author. Hola, that is I.

Journeying through life and tumbling across thought, as we all do, I wished to cross the Ts and book them, ergo them's're booked.

23:10, 19%.. 46 minutes remaining? I doubt that, never trust a computer on time.

I blame my scattered thoughts for mumbling. Power saving, kicked in, swell.

I procrastinate (thank you spel check).

My poems are precious to me and if that is the let alone target, I would rest easy. Though I feel uneasy calling these poems, I feel they have no external value, extreme internal meaning and value, but to all else outside my mind, I market them at the current price of a Pepe token, £0.00001291 (psudodyslexia really does not help counting zeros.. good L*rd, I hope crypto sky rockets).

23:22, 14%, 36 minutes remain.. does that add up? Maybe I was wrong.

I do adore poetry, it is a pleasant form of art and I find it an ease of access to envisage my thoughts. I am only witness to my own testimony and can only testify to my sole soul witness. Don't think too hard on that, totally makes sense.

I do not expect any much more than as to picture my wandered, alluded and captured thoughts, my mindful chatter, no more than taking a meaningful picture on an iPhone, obviously, and printing it to frame.

Pfft, absolutely knew it, 4% remai

Pranks,

I should probably take up another hobby like rug collecting or plane spotting

Or

perchance (so poetic) I'll shed another few pages of gatheredness.

.. which is definitely a word, in trust we shall not look it up.

Peaceful affairs,

Booker.

www.ingramcontent.com/pod-product-compliance
Lightning Source LLC
Chambersburg PA
CBHW070340120526
44590CB00017B/2957